Writing for Virtual Reality

Innovative Storytelling Techniques in a Digital Age

Table of Contents

Chapter 1. Introduction

As we catapult headfirst into the digital age, the way we consume stories continues to evolve at an exhilarating pace. Our Special Report, "Writing for Virtual Reality: Innovative Storytelling Techniques in a Digital Age", delves into this exhilarating evolution, exploring how writers are using breakthrough technology to create immersive experiences like never before. This comprehensive guide to the cutting-edge landscape of VR storytelling will captivate you with a wealth of revolutionary techniques and innovative narratives. It's the perfect mix of insightful knowledge, inspiration, and practical advice. Whether you're a seasoned storyteller or new to the digital world, this report is an invaluable asset, shedding light on opportunities to captivate audiences in ways we only dreamt possible a few years ago. Let's embark on this exciting journey together, opening the door to a vibrant new world of storytelling!

Chapter 2. The Dawn of Virtual Reality Storytelling

The advent of virtual reality (VR) sparked a new epoch in media, revolutionizing the way we interact with and consume stories. It presents us with an unparalleled medium that fuses traditional narrative structures with immersive, sensory experiences. This leap in storytelling devices has offered writers an innovative palette of techniques to draw on, creating a ripple effect extending far beyond the realm of VR itself.

2.1. The Birth of a New Medium

In the mid-twentieth century, when the first traces of VR were conceptualized, few anticipated the narrative implications of this technology. Inventors like Morton Heilig, who patented the first VR Head-Mounted Display (HMD) in 1962, were driven by the desire to create a more immersive film-going experience.

Fast forward to today, VR storytelling is a dynamic field where traditional narrative structures intertwine with interactive, sensory-driven experiences. Mundane activities become adventures, historical events transform into personal experiences, and simple stories morph into immersive journeys.

2.2. Literature and Cinema's Influences on VR Storytelling

No narrative language emerges in a vacuum, and VR storytelling is no exception. It draws heavily from the narrative structures established by literature and cinema. In VR, it's not enough to see or hear the story - the viewer must 'be' in the story.

While cinema has long played with the notion of subjective camera positions, VR took the concept a step further, integrating the viewer into the midst of the story. And literary influences can be seen in the ways that VR can tap into the individual sensory and emotional experiences, akin to the reader immersing themselves in a novel.

2.3. The New Rules of Engagement

With VR storytelling, the narrative starts as soon as the headset goes on. Therefore, the scene-setting and character introduction, traditionally taken care of in the first few pages of a book or opening scenes of a movie, already need to have occurred. A character's backstory may be revealed through a physical object, a sound hinting at prior events, or the environment speaking to past occurrences.

Unlike traditional linear storytelling, where the writer controls the pacing and sequence of events, VR engages users in an active part of the narrative. They decide where to look, when to interact, and how to move. The writer's job is to design a narrative that accommodates these choices, crafting different narrative elements within the environment that the viewer can control to some extent.

2.4. Navigating the Challenges that VR Poses

Despite the unparalleled possibilities that VR offers, it presents its own set of challenges. VR has to contend with technical limitations such as viewer discomfort, motion sickness, and the lack of a standardized interface. From a narrative standpoint, VR also struggles with issues like fragmented attention, as viewers have the freedom to look anywhere they want, making it tough to focus their attention on the narrative's key elements.

As a result, writers need to craft their narratives in a way that guides the viewer's gaze in subtle ways, focusing their attention where it's needed in the narrative while avoiding alienation by being too forceful.

2.5. The Future of VR Storytelling

In the coming years, we can expect to see more experiments incorporating AI into VR narratives, forming unique, user-personalized experiences. This advancement could even allow for stories that evolve and unfold differently for each user, based upon their response to different stimuli within the VR environment.

Such developments will expand the narrative potential of VR storytelling, bringing us closer to an era where storytelling isn't just about listening or watching, but truly about 'being'.

In the whirlwind of these exciting advancements, writers now find themselves on the forefront of a narrative revolution. The traditional role of the writer is transforming, requiring them not just to tell stories, but to craft worlds and guide experiencers through them. It's no longer just about the narrative arc, but the comprehensive journey that each experiencer can embark upon.

In the wake of technological advancements, the writer is becoming an enabler of experiences. The written word remains the foundation of all stories, but writers must now learn to incorporate unconventional, sensory cues into their storytelling toolkit to fully tap into the possibilities of VR. Their role has expanded beyond traditional narrative boundaries, converging towards that of a world-builder, a guide, and an experiential maestro.

As VR continues to redefine the digital age and enrich our storytelling practices, writers need to keep pace with the shifting landscape. The dawn of VR storytelling is not merely an exciting transition, but a profound exploration of our narrative capabilities, opening unforeseen avenues for writers worldwide. Buckle up, for the future of storytelling is now, and it is embodied in the immersive world of VR!

Chapter 3. Technological Advances Shaping VR Narratives

In the realm of Virtual Reality (VR), the rapid technological advancements are facilitating novel forms of storytelling. Technology fuelling VR narratives ranges across multiple dimensions including interactive hardware, developing software, and protocols for constructing immersive experiences.

3.1. Hardware Innovations

The most substantial component that shapes VR narratives is undoubtedly the hardware. Initially, VR hardware was costly, cumbersome, and offered limited capabilities. Now, however, vast technological strides have simplified designs, cut costs, and exponentially expanded possibilities.

Head-Mounted Displays (HMDs), augmented with motion sensors, form the backbone of VR environments. Brands such as Oculus, HTC, and Sony have produced HMDs like Oculus Rift, HTC Vive, and PlayStation VR. These have superior resolution screens, latency and refresh rates, providing a seamless, realistic, and immersive VR experience.

Advanced VR gear includes gloves and suits equipped with haptic feedback. This simulates the touch and feel of a virtual world, deepening the immersive experience. An essential player, Teslasuit, offers full-body haptic suits, bringing distinct physical layers of VR to life.

VR peripherals are broadening to include items like 3D spatial controllers, treadmills and more. Companies like 3DRudder, with their VR foot motion controller and Virtuix Omni's omnidirectional treadmill, are giving users novel interactional roles in VR narratives by enabling natural movement and control.

Lastly, the strides in wireless technologies and advanced processing capabilities are freeing audiences from cables and heavy processing units. The standalone VR headset, Oculus Quest, for example, offers the freedom to move without tethering cables which deepens the immersion and allows for expansive narrative choices.

3.2. Software Developments

Parallel to the hardware, software innovations enable more sophisticated VR narratives. High-quality graphics, physics engines, and responsive AI, deeply affect how we consume VR narratives.

Unity and Unreal Engine, two prominent VR development platforms, offer developers a suite of tools to create compelling narratives. This includes realistic graphical rendering capabilities, life-like physics simulation, and customizable artificial intelligence behaviour, all of which power the core interactive elements of VR storytelling.

Improvement in graphics rendering technology like Ray Tracing, enables one to create photorealistic environments. It simulates light's behaviour, creating accurate reflections, refractions, and shadows in real-time. This advancement fosters richer, more credible VR environments, making narratives more captivating.

Physics simulations make interactions within VR environments believable. Sophisticated engines replicate real-world physics – gravity, momentum, fluid dynamics, all of which anchor the user in the narrative by providing a familiar, tangible context.

Machine Learning (ML) and Artificial Intelligence (AI) are shaping interactive NPCs (Non-Player Characters) within VR narratives. Characters can respond and adapt to a user's actions uniquely, keeping storylines fresh and unpredictable. AI has the potential to generate dynamic narratives where the story adapts to the user's choices, making each playthrough a different experience.

3.3. Protocols for Constructing Immersive Experiences

The hardware and software innovations are meaningless without well-crafted VR narratives. Traditionally, storytellers could control their content completely. By contrast, VR environments give control to the audience, letting them explore at their pace.

This interactive feature means traditional linear narratives may not engage VR audiences satisfyingly. Hence, new storytelling protocols like the use of 'Spatial Narrative', which leverages the environment to tell the story, are gaining popularity. Developers are innovatively designing their VR spaces to subconsciously guide the user's attention to pivotal story elements while retaining the sense of freedom essential in VR narratives.

Similarly, 'Environmental Storytelling' and 'Embedded Narrative' are techniques where the narrative is imbibed into the environment. Developers subtly ingrain details into the scene which the audience can interpret and uncover sequentially, hence experiencing a unique personal narrative.

With immersive audio simulating 360-degree spaces, VR narratives are also harnessing music and sound as powerful storytelling tools. Binaural and ambisonic audio add depth to the scene, helping navigate the user's attention to narrative elements.

Finally, choice and consequence systems present audiences with moral and strategic decisions that alter the story's course, thereby making them active participators in shaping the narrative.

In conclusion, the technologies driving VR narratives are developing at a breathtaking pace. Optimizing the interplay between hardware, software, and narrative techniques is critical to crafting immersive VR stories. The fusion of interactive, immersive 3D worlds with compelling narratives presents an exciting frontier for storytelling, forever altering how we consume and produce narratives.

Chapter 4. The Role of Interactivity in VR Storytelling

Interactivity has always played a crucial role in storytelling, enabling audiences to engage with the narrative in profound ways. With the advent of virtual reality (VR), storytellers now have a game-changing tool at their disposal that could entirely alter the traditional ways of telling a story. This chapter explores the distinctive aspects of VR storytelling, primarily focusing on the pivotal role of interactivity.

4.1. Expanding the Definition of Interactivity

VR storytelling extends the conventional understanding of interactivity, evolving beyond simple click-through stories or choose-your-own-adventure games. In the VR paradigm, interactivity is not just about making decisions that influence narrative progression. It's about 'presence' - the feeling of actually existing within the story world.

In VR, audiences can physically perceive and explore their environment. They can hold objects, talk to characters, even change the scene's tempo. This '360-degree' experience can have a profound impact on audiences, allowing them to embody the narrative, rather than just passively watching it unfold. In a sense, VR blurs the line between the storyteller and the audience, as the latter becomes an integral part of the narrative - a shift that is both fascinating and challenging for writers.

4.2. Bridging the Gap between Passive and Active Engagement

In traditional media, passive engagement means absorbing a story without real interaction, while active engagement allows audiences to influence the narrative. VR storytelling, however, exists somewhere between these two extremes.

On one hand, VR viewers can explore the narrative world at their own pace, without the typical constraints of linear narratives. On the other hand, they are still guided by the storyteller, who designs the environment, sets the narrative goals, and leads the viewer towards them.

Therefore, VR writers have to strike a balance between giving audiences agency and maintaining narrative control. This is achieved through clever use of interactivity: immersive environments that encourage exploration; dynamic events that captivate attention; physical interactions that make the viewer feel part of the story world.

4.3. The Mechanics of Interaction

Designing interactions in VR goes beyond scripting and animation; it becomes a matter of spatial design and user experience. A fundamental principle shared by most VR writers is to design interactions that feel natural to the viewer.

Imagine a detective story. Instead of passively watching events unfold, viewers can actively observe the crime scene, pick up clues, even question witnesses. The primary storytelling mechanic is no longer the narrator's voice; it's the viewer's curiosity and actions. Viewers feel more engaged because they have an active role in the spatiotemporal unfolding of the narrative.

4.4. The Narrative Significance of Interactivity

Interactivity in VR isn't just a tool for immersion; it can be a narrative method in itself. Certain information or plot developments could be revealed based on the viewer's actions or explorations. For example, a war story where the viewer plays a soldier: their actions determine the soldiers they save, the battles they win, and ultimately, the plot progression.

Direct interactivity also allows viewers to feel the consequences of their choices, engendering a deeper emotional investment in the narrative. This affective power of interactivity in VR storytelling is something traditional storytelling methods simply cannot replicate.

4.5. The Art of Guiding Interactions

Getting viewers to engage with the environment is one thing; leading them through the story is another. VR storytellers must find ways to guide the viewers' actions to ensure narrative progression.

Environmental cues, like lighting or sound, can grab viewers' attention, leading them to significant areas or events. Characters' behavior or visual symbols can provide hints about what actions to perform. Unforeseen events can limit their freedom, pushing them in certain directions or shaping their choices.

However, this requires a delicate balance. Overly directive cues could make viewers feel restricted, while too subtle ones could lead to confusion. The art of interactivity in VR storytelling is about giving viewers enough agency to immerse themselves while also directing their actions to tell a satisfying story.

4.6. Interactivity and Connectedness

Finally, the emergence of social VR provides interesting perspectives for our understanding of interactivity in VR storytelling. Imagine being able to share a VR narrative with others, exploring the story world together, discussing the narrative events, and influencing the storyline collectively.

This form of interactivity adds a new layer of complexity to VR storytelling. The viewers are not only interacting with the narrative and environment; they are also interacting with each other. They can collaborate or compete; they can witness the consequences of not just their actions but also those of others.

Through this expansive exploration into interactivity in VR storytelling, it becomes clear that the exciting evolution of VR augments traditional storytelling techniques. VR powers interactivity, simulation, and engagement, providing the viewer with new ways to experience narratives. A careful understanding of these concepts is therefore crucial for any writer hoping to enter this exciting realm.

Chapter 5. Writing Techniques for Immersive Experiences

The line separating reality and fiction blurs as storytelling evolves with the latest technology. Enhanced viewer experiences and unmatched audience immersion are now at the forefront, courtesy of Virtual Reality (VR). This digital revolution, however, requires a novel approach and an understanding of how traditional narrative techniques adapt in VR settings.

5.1. Understanding Immersive Storytelling

Before diving into writing techniques, it's vital to understand immersive storytelling's basics in a VR context. Unlike conventional narrative methods where a tale unfolds linearly, immersive storytelling in VR revolves around creating a believable virtual world. Here, your audience can influence the narrative and interact with the surrounding. It notches up the spectrum of storytelling, breaking free from the traditional boundaries of passive consumption.

5.2. First-Person Perspective is Key

The essence of VR storytelling is rooted in the first-person viewpoint. It's crucial to consider this change in narrative perspective when developing a VR story. Traditional third-person perspective limits the audience to the outsider's view, impeding immersion. However, shifting to first-person perspective transforms the audience from mere observers to active participants.

Write your story as if the viewer is the protagonist, engaging directly with the environment and characters. The storyline should allow viewers to react naturally, enhancing their sense of presence in your narrative.

5.3. Explore Non-Linear Storytelling

In conventional storytelling, the story follows a neatly ordered sequence - beginning, middle, end. With VR, it's a different ballgame as VR is inherently non-linear. This type of storytelling encourages the audience to explore the narrative in their own time, and in their own way based on their interactions within the VR world.

Throw out the old rule book when designing a narrative structure for VR storytelling. Instead of structuring your story in a sequence, consider it as an environment waiting to be explored. You can plant narrative elements throughout the virtual landscape for viewers to discover as they navigate the scene, giving them a unique sense of autonomy and engagement.

5.4. Define the Audience's Role Clearly

Does your viewer have an invisible presence, or are they an active character within the plot? Are they mere observers or can they influence the outcome of the story? These are questions you should address at the start of your narrative design.

Consider how the viewer's role impacts the interaction within the virtual world - how they perceive their environment, the characters, and the events that unfold. The audience's self-perception in VR adds depth to their experience and boosts immersion.

5.5. Designing the Environment

The environment is not just a backdrop in VR; it's an essential part of the story. Leverage it to further your narrative, deepen immersion and engage your audience more thoroughly. A well-crafted environment can guide your audience's attention and hint at plot developments.

Pay attention to every detail, from the atmosphere to the lighting, props, color palette, sound design and more. Each of these elements subconsciously influences the viewer's interpretation of the narrative.

5.6. Creating Empathy with Characters

Emotion fuels engagement. When viewers are emotionally invested in your characters, they embrace the overall storyline more willingly. In VR, character empathy can be amplified by leveraging visual cues, dialogue, and the characters' reactions to the viewer's actions. Remember, the audience isn't just watching your characters, they're sharing experiences with them in this immersive world.

5.7. Challenges & Solutions in VR Storytelling

Writing for VR presents an array of challenges. Perhaps the most daunting is the absence of a defined frame for storytelling. Unlike film or theatre, you cannot control exactly where your audience will look at any given moment, which can make delivering key information a challenge.

To mitigate this uncertainty, employ multi-sensory cues to guide your audience toward critical elements in your story. Sound, light, and characters' actions can all work together to subtly guide your viewers in the right direction.

5.8. Wrap Up

VR storytelling is an exciting and ever-evolving medium, and the above techniques offer a solid foundation. Experiment, be open to new possibilities, forge your unique style, and above all, keep the audience's experience at the heart of your creation. These tips should provide the terminology and understanding needed to confidently step into the world of VR storytelling, where the lines between reality and fantasy become wonderfully blurred.

Chapter 6. Character Development in a Virtual World

Understanding and crafting characters is central to the art of storytelling. In traditional media, this involves understanding a character's motivations, growth, and evolution throughout the narrative. The advent of Virtual Reality (VR) brings this dynamic process to a whole new level. In VR, characters don't just exist around the narrative; they have the potential to shape and be a part of the experience in a more compelling way.

6.1. The Evolution of Characters in VR

Historically, characters were defined by their actions and words within the limits of a page or screen. With VR, there's a shift from observing characters, to interacting and engaging with them in a multidimensional way. In VR, characters can respond to the user's actions, creating a distinct sense of immersive experience; as though the user is a part of the narrative, thus, fostering meaningful relationships between the user and the character.

Virtual reality constructs a spatial medium where a character's physicality is crucial. How they physically exist and how they interact with their surroundings adds a layer of depth that brings them alive. Their movements, positioning, body language, even silences, stimulate a sense of tangibility. Consequently, the creator must pay special attention to the physicality and mannerisms of characters in VR.

6.2. Crafting Characters in VR

Creating compelling characters for VR includes traditional narrative methods, as well as exploiting the unique elements of VR technology. It's an exercise in understanding complex human behaviour, psychology, as well as intricate technological aspects.

1. **Physical Presence**: Physical presence, or body language, can be used to create a stronger relationship between the user and the character. For instance, when a character physically leans towards the user or maintains eye contact, it creates an undeniably powerful connection.

2. **Interactivity**: Interactivity can influence the depth of relationship with the protagonist. Even simple actions such as a character responding to head movements or hand gestures can significantly affect the narrative.

3. **Voice**: Giving a character a voice adds another level of depth, making them seem more real. It works wonders in portraying a character's emotions, making their reactions believable.

4. **Mannerisms**: Distinct quirks and personal tics make characters unique, aiding in distinguishing them from one another in the virtual environment.

6.3. Establishing Relationships

The level of intimacy established between the user and the character can significantly influence the storytelling experience. Moving beyond merely observing, users can now sympathise, empathise, and even build amity or animosity with characters. Therefore, writers must find ways to encourage this relationship dynamically.

1. **Vulnerability**: Characters revealing their insecurities can foster a bond with the user. Showing a scar, narrating a story of past hurt, or sharing a weakness can make characters relatable and more

human.

2. **Responsivity**: Characters that respond to the user's actions can create incredible immersion. A character that recognizes and echoes the user's emotional state aids in developing a strong connection.

3. **Rapport**: A character that establishes a rapport with the user by initiating conversations or expressing shared interests deepens engagement.

6.4. Challenges and Solutions

Creating efficient characters for VR isn't without its challenges. Two main issues are Uncanny Valley and the matter of User-Character Consistency.

Uncanny Valley describes a phenomenon where an almost-human-looking avatar turns out to be disturbing or creepy. The solution lies in intentional design; to show that this character is an 'other', making use of stylization or exemplifying certain non-human traits.

User-Character Consistency becomes uncertain in an immersive experience such as VR. How do you ensure that actions taken by the user align with the character's personality or behaviour? One solution is to provide consistent feedback, shaping the user's actions in line with the character's persona and narrative arc.

6.5. Conclusion

Character Development in a VR World is an intricate and enriching process that revolves around creating engaging, relatable, and interactive experiences. VR technology provides writers and creators with an array of tools and techniques to bring characters to life in a vividly immersive environment.

As we continue to explore this realm, our understanding of virtual characters will grow. Moreover, it will refine the art of virtual storytelling, fostering relationships between users and virtual characters that are meaningful and impactful.

This journey into character development within VR is just the beginning. The unprecedented opportunities for creativity and invention pave the way for a vibrant new era in storytelling.

Chapter 7. Creating Compelling Settings in VR

The journey of storytelling in VR begins with the setting. Immersing a user in a believable environment translates into high-quality and deeply engaging VR experiences. A key point to note is this: convincing settings aren't just visual spectacles; they should nurture the story and stimulate interactivity.

7.1. Understanding the Role of Settings in VR

Traditionally, settings have been backgrounds against which events unfold. In VR, settings become playgrounds — they are interactive, dynamic, mutable and integral to the narrative. In fact, they can themselves become characters. A haunted house could send a shiver down one's spine, a vibrant city could pulse with life, a spaceship could hum with alien energy — all evoking emotional responses in the onlooker.

7.2. The Basics of Setting Creation

To create convincing settings:

1. Understand the story: The setting should effectively facilitate and complement the narrative. Therefore, understanding the mood, tone, and events of the story is crucial.

2. Detail Planning: Outlining every visual, auditory, and interactive detail of the setting will pave the way for a cohesive virtual environment.

3. Engage all senses: VR allows for a multidimensional experience. So, try to engage as many senses as possible. Besides sight and

sound, tactility and even smell can be incorporated, amplifying the level of immersion.

7.3. The Power of Immersion

The goal of VR is to make the user forget about the real world that they inhabit. Conjuring a potent mix of visual grandiosity, evocative audio, and seamless interactivity can mask the sense of reality efficiently.

1. Visual Immersion: Striving for photorealistic environments can enhance the feeling of being in a different 'real' place. However, don't dismiss stylized or simplified graphics; they can still foster immersion if they are used consistently and constructively.

2. Auditory Immersion: Soundscapes carry a potent emotional punch. From subtle ambient sounds to emphatic sound effects, it is imperative to craft a rich sound design.

3. Interactive Immersion: Empower the user to create changes in the environment. This induces a feeling of agency and makes the VR experience more compelling.

7.4. Creating 3-Dimensional Spaces

With VR, you're not presenting a stage to your audience; you're placing them in the middle of the action.

1. Scale and Perspective: VR settings should have depth and dimensions. Using perspective to your advantage can invoke feelings of awe, dread, or tranquility.

2. Navigation and Movement: Movement in VR should feel natural. Whether it's teleportation-based or free roam, it must be intuitive and comfortable to prevent motion sickness.

3. Spatial Sound: This is 3-dimensional sound that changes

depending on the user's location and orientation. This adds another layer of depth to the world, making it feel all the more real.

7.5. Continuity and Exploration

Maintain continuity in your settings as well as encourage user exploration.

1. Continuity: Ensure that the visual, temporal, and spatial aspects consistently relate to the narrative and each other. Discrepancy can be jarring and rupture the sense of immersion.

2. Exploration: Encourage users to explore the environment. Hints of a past event, shadowy corners holding surprises, or easter eggs can compel the user to delve deeper into the VR world.

7.6. Physical Interaction

Interaction with objects forms a substantial part of the VR experience.

1. Sensible Interactions: Each interaction should make sense in relation to the narrative, and be smoothly executed without hindrance.

2. Realistic Physics: Real-world physics should be used as a reference to simulate interactions. Unless deliberately tweaked for narrative purposes, objects should behave as expected in real life.

3. Interactive Objects: These should be easily distinguishable and intuitive to operate.

7.7. Developing a Distinct Atmosphere

A multidimensional, harmonic orchestra of light, sound, color, texture, and movement can concoct a distinct atmosphere. This atmosphere could induce feelings pertinent to the narrative, influence the pacing, and guide the user's attention.

7.8. Conclusion

The creation of compelling settings in VR storytelling is a complex process that requires a meticulous understanding of the medium. Spaces are no longer passive; instead, they are imbued with life, becoming a fundamental part of the narrative structure. The settings invite exploration, breed immersion, and convert the audience into active participants. A compelling setting can enrich a VR story, transforming it from a fleeting experience to an unforgettable journey.

Remember, in VR, our only true constraint is the limitless realm of our own imagination. It's time to roll up your sleeves and get creating!

Chapter 8. The Impact of VR on Audience Engagement

In the digital age, Virtual Reality (VR) has emerged as a revolutionary force, redefining how we perceive, interact with, and are emotionally affected by content. This inaugural section delves into the profound impact VR has had on audience engagement, reshaping the ways stories are told and experienced.

8.1. Transforming Passive Spectators into Active Participants

Traditionally, consuming a story meant sitting back passively, letting the narrative wash over us without any direct influence on how it unfolds. However, VR radically blurs the lines between fiction and reality by transforming passive spectators into active participants in the virtual realm. Now, it's not just about 'viewing' the story, but rather 'being a part' and 'living' in it.

By immersing audiences directly inside the story and allowing them to interact with their surroundings, VR can evoke vastly different emotions and reactions compared to more passive mediums like books, films, or TV shows. This pioneering shift from passive spectatorship to active involvement offers a profound reimagining of audience engagement, granting participants a unique agency that dramatically alters the narrative's emotional and experiential dimension.

8.2. The Confluence of Immersion and Presence

One of the most distinguishing factors of VR storytelling is the profound sense of immersion and presence it cultivates. Immersion refers to the technology's ability to present a believable alternative reality through sight and sound. Simultaneously, presence describes the viewer's subjective experience, indicating the extent to which they feel part of the virtual environment.

Together, these elements contribute to an intensified engagement, tying the audience emotionally and cognitively more tightly to the unfolding narrative. Not only can the viewers look around and interact with the virtual world, but the finely tuned sensory stimuli — such as 360-degree vision or even tactile feedback — can help make the viewers forget they are experiencing a simulation at all.

8.3. The Embodiment of Characters

Virtual reality further takes advantage of avatar embodiment, enabling participants to step into the shoes of the characters and directly experience their perspectives. This transformative power of embodying characters marks a leap beyond merely empathizing with them. Understanding a character's motivations and struggles becomes significantly more personal and profound when an audience member experiences those struggles from within.

By stepping into someone else's life or even time, VR storytelling can transcend traditional limits of imagination, empathy, and understanding. Furthermore, this engagement might have a lasting, real-world influence, embedding new viewpoints and perspectives that extend beyond the shared experience in the virtual world.

8.4. Introducing Branching Narratives

VR storytelling introduces the concept of branching narratives, which gives audiences an active role to shape the story's trajectory. These decision-based storylines offer multiple outcomes based on users' decisions and actions, paving the way for unique, personalized stories that yield a deeper level of engagement.

This narrative approach is reminiscent of the 'choose your own adventure' books, but with the added benefits of full immersion and interactivity that come with VR. The concept of branching narratives ultimately realizes the age-old fantasy of "living a story", offering audiences a greater sense of control and involvement in the storyline.

8.5. Engaging Beyond Entertainment

While we've focused on entertainment thus far, the scope of VR's immersive potential extends far beyond that. From educational scenarios, training simulations to therapeutic applications, VR has the capability to engage audiences and invoke tangible change in real-world behavior and perceptions.

For example, in an educational setting, VR offers students immersive, firsthand experiences that can make complex concepts come alive. When learners dive headfirst into the Amazon rainforest or walk the streets of Ancient Rome, they engage more deeply with the learning material, thereby bolstering understanding and retention.

Meanwhile, VR can serve as a potent tool for empathy-building, exposing people to different perspectives, and experiences they might never encounter in their daily lives. Experiencing the life of a refugee or understanding the impacts of climate change becomes imminently more powerful through the full sensory and emotional engagement that VR provides. The storytelling power of VR is uniquely able to create deep connections, stir powerful emotions, and compel viewers to action.

The world of VR storytelling continues to unfold, driven by not only technological advancements but also the creativity and courage of writers and creators daring to push traditional narrative boundaries. By placing audiences directly within the narrative, VR storytelling transforms the fundamental dynamics between stories, their creators, and audiences. With its ability to merge immersion, interactivity, and impactful storytelling, VR promises to continue its trajectory as a particular force in audience engagement. The digital age has only just begun to uncover what's possible.

Chapter 9. Case Studies: Successful VR Narratives

In the world of Virtual Reality (VR) narratives, there have been some standout successes that encapsulate the potential of this immersive storytelling platform. The following case studies exemplify the extraordinary strides taken in the VR landscape, demonstrating ingenious uses of the technology and innovative approaches to storytelling.

9.1. Case Study 1: The Invisible Hours

""*The Invisible Hours*" is a prime example of a successful VR narrative. As an immersive theatre experience developed by Tequila Works, it blurs the line between video game and film, allowing its audience to watch a murder mystery unfold in a real-time 3D environment.

The narrative unravels across various locations at different times, meaning the users can choose where to be and when—essentially becoming omnipresent. They have the liberty of following any character, combing through rooms, or waiting around corners to uncover the storyline. This experimental model enhances immersive storytelling, instigating an entirely unprecedented form of audience engagement.

9.2. Case Study 2: Dear Angelica

"*Dear Angelica*" is another pinnacle in VR narratives, brought to life by Oculus Story Studio. It pairs a poignant narrative with beautiful, hand-drawn visuals created entirely in VR using the Quill tool.

This unique approach in using VR to illustrate the story rather than just deploying it for immersion enhances the emotional attachment between the audience and narrative. The freehand-drawn art creates an intimate, dream-like atmosphere, and the user feels they're entering the narrator's personal thoughts and memories.

9.3. Case Study 3: Accounting+

An entirely different take on VR storytelling is seen in the comedy-adventure game, ""Accounting+", developed by Crows Crows Crows and Squanch Games. This narrative uses improvisation as its cornerstone, making most of its content an unpredictable, hilarious montage.

What makes this narrative so compelling is its expert mix of unpredictability with the magic of VR interactivity. The user gets an unfiltered view of this wacky universe and is instrumental in driving the story forward, ultimately tailoring each playthrough to be a unique, humorous endeavor.

9.4. Case Study 4: Vader Immortal

"Vader Immortal," a star-wars themed VR series by ILMxLAB, is a masterful blend of cinematic storytelling and interactive gameplay. By thrusting the user into a well-loved universe, the narrative creates an immediate connection with the audience.

There is abundant use of active participation, like using lightsabers and engaging in starship battles, which amps up the narrative thrills. But the true success lies in successfully integrating these gameplay elements seamlessly within the storytelling framework.

9.5. Case Study 5: The Under Presents

Tender Claws Studio's ""*The Under Presents*", combines VR with live theatre, blurring the boundary between audience and performer. Users can interact not only with the environment but also react to live actors present in the virtual space.

The narrative's true triumph lies in this innovative approach, mixing live theater techniques with VR interactivity, carving out a niche in immersive storytelling. The user is thrown into unexpected situations, creating a rare, enchanting narrative, making it a unique case study in VR storytelling.

These cases exemplify the vast potential VR narratives hold. From deploying artwork, comedy, acclaimed classics, live theater to innovating omnipresence, these narratives each bring something unique to the table. As VR technology advances, the horizon for immersive storytelling will continue expanding, offering storytellers a surreal, uncharted platform to captivate audiences like never before.

Each case study successfully showcases how VR's inherent immersivity can be united with compelling narratives, leading to a profound storytelling experience. The techniques and insights drawn from these cases can help future developers and creators conceive innovative narratives, shaping the course of immersive storytelling, and redefining it for the future.

Chapter 10. Challenges and Solutions in VR Writing

Understanding the applications, limitations, and challenges of Virtual Reality (VR) is the first step towards harnessing its potential to offer fascinating stories. It's essential to ponder these hurdles, and even more crucial to propose creative and ingenuous solutions, facilitating a smooth transition from traditional storytelling to this ultra-modern technology.

10.1. The Challenge of Physical Discomfort

One of the significant challenges in VR writing is the potential for users to experience physical discomfort, such as motion sickness, while using the VR equipment. Despite having a captivating story, an uncomfortable user will quickly disengage, nullifying all narrative and immersion efforts.

In solving the issue of physical discomfort, developers have been making use of "comfort design" principles. These principles look to minimize the amount of motion the user undergoes in the VR environment, maintaining a standard of comfort. While these constraints can limit the freedom to roam in a VR narrative, clever writing that incorporates these principles can turn them into opportunities for deeper immersion.

10.2. Dimensional Dialogue: A New Frontier

Writing dialogue for VR experiences introduces an entirely new level of immersion, but also its own set of challenges. Traditional dialogue seen in games and films usually depends on cut scenes or shot-reverse-shot techniques to emphasize characters' reactions. These techniques fall short in VR, as there's no cut scene or frame to concentrate on the intended visual focus.

Writers, therefore, need to adapt their approach to dialogue. They can place narrative threads throughout the VR environment, prompting the user to interact with objects or characters to expose these threads. This immersive dialogue can create a dynamic and reactive environment, but it requires writers to consider context and experience on a whole new level.

10.3. The Technology: A Double-Edged Sword

While cutting-edge technology is what enables VR storytelling, it also imposes restrictions. Different VR headsets offer different features, and there's a constant need to adapt and update experiences as technology progresses. This can limit a writer's creative freedom, forcing them to ensure their stories are compatible and functional on each technological platform.

However, worries over technological compatibility don't mean that authors have to stifle their creativity. By maintaining an understanding of the VR landscape, they can create stories that make the most out of current technology, offering engaging narratives within limited hardware and software capabilities. In this sense, the technology barrier is a challenge, but also an opportunity to innovate and experiment.

10.4. Linearity vs. Interactivity: The Narrative Balance

Balancing linearity and interactivity is a unique challenge of VR writing. On one hand, too much linearity can limit a user's sense of agency and immersion. On the other hand, high interactivity can result in a loss of narrative control, making the story convoluted or even inaccessible.

It's essential, then, to hit a narrative sweet spot. Use limited linearity to guide the user through the story, and ample interactivity to make the experience immersive and engaging. This process can be intricate, requiring a deep understanding of the medium, but the payoff is worth it: a perfectly balanced VR narrative is unlike any other storytelling experience.

10.5. Developing a Writer's Toolkit for VR

Technological advances and new mediums necessitate the evolution of the writing craft. In the context of VR, writing tools used for film or literature might not always be effective. Consequently, writers must explore, experiment, and create a whole new set of tools specific to VR.

This development can seem daunting, yet it's an exciting opportunity for those bold enough to venture into this new territory. Writers can blend different techniques to find strategies that work best for them – such as spatial storytelling, environmental clues, and innovative dialogue mechanics – resulting in a unique toolkit for the VR medium.

In conclusion, despite the various challenges VR writing presents, they are not insurmountable. With creative thinking, adaption, and maintaining a balance between traditional and new-age writing techniques, writers can rise above these issues. As we continue to navigate through the digital age, the potential of VR storytelling is only limited by our imagination. With the correct tools, this technology can become an immersive landscape for narratives, fostering a new era of storytelling.

Chapter 11. Looking Forward: The Future of VR Storytelling

The constant march of technological progress ensures that the realm of storytelling, too, remains in fluid flux, ever-evolving, and as digital trends shift into virtual reality, we find ourselves standing before a portal to unprecedented possibilities. Looking ahead raises questions as much as it excites the imagination. Who is in charge of these narratives and how will they evolve? What new forms of interaction are possible? Thus, we dive headfirst into the era of VR storytelling.

11.1. The Storytellers of Tomorrow

In a time not long ago, only trained professionals hailing from disciplines such as cinema, game design, or literature penned the material which would later form the foundations for VR narratives. Today, this scenario is shifting. As VR tech becomes increasingly accessible and democratized, a growing pool of creators is emerging, each riding a unique wave of creativity.

New digital tools are making it possible for anyone with a story to tell to bring it vividly to life. These entry-level platforms are easy-to-use, irrespective of your tech prowess, adding a creative dimension to the art of storytelling. This heightened access will significantly determine the shape of VR narratives in the future, as more diverse voices add to the cacophony of virtual reality.

11.2. Interaction and Immersion

The interactivity in VR storytelling is undergoing a transformation as well. Traditional forms of interaction like controllers and keyboards give way to more intuitive, natural forms of communication within the digital realm, including voice and gesture commands. This evolution brings narrative and gameplay experiences closer to the actions and responses in real-life conditions, thereby augmenting our connection to the story being told.

Another notable shift is the movement towards dynamic storytelling elements. Today, we witness the emergence of AI-driven interactive narratives that evolve based on user interactions. Soon, we could have stories where no two experiences are the same. This evolution propels us into a future where stories become delightful gardens to explore, rather than fixed paths to follow.

11.3. Sensory Augmentation

Future VR experiences aim not only to trick the sight and sound but to adequately serve all the senses. This concept of 'full sensory VR' will replicate conditions of touch, taste, smell and feel, creating the illusion of the story playing out "for real". By fooling our brains into accepting virtual scenarios as actual experiences, this technique invites a deeper degree of empathy and immersion, revolutionising the storytelling game.

11.4. Infrastructure and Accessibility

The growth and sustainability of VR storytelling heavily rest on two crucial pillars: robust infrastructure and wider accessibility. Currently, high-quality VR experiences require substantial computational power, which can be an entry barrier for many. However, with the advent of solutions like cloud-based rendering, VR platforms are taking large strides forward to become more accessible.

The availability of affordable VR equipment, coupled with a steady inflow of impressive content, will sustain the growth of the VR user base. A broad and varied audience is as essential to the future of VR storytelling as the storytellers themselves.

11.5. Biofeedback and Adaptive Narratives

Imagine a story that not only responds to your choices and actions but also understands and reacts to your complex emotional and physical state. Biofeedback technology in VR narratives analyzes data such as the user's heart-rate, skin temperature, and stress levels, enabling the storyline to adapt based on the emotional state of the user. This could make for truly transpersonal experiences, allowing an unprecedented level of immersion.

11.6. The Challenges Ahead

While the prospects of VR storytelling excite us, challenges persist. First, there is the substantial question of user safety and emotional well-being. The closer we get to simulating reality, the grimmer the ethical implications.

Secondly, given the increasing democratization of VR storytelling, how do we ensure that the narratives produced are of substantial quality and contribute positively to the diversity of human experiences?

These are just a glimpse of the obstacles that lie ahead. Nevertheless, it is undeniable that VR storytelling holds immense promise.

The future of VR storytelling can thus materialize as a dynamic, ever-evolving landscape, a testament to the joint efforts of technology and creative minds. As we move forward, narratives won't just be about telling stories; they would also involve living them in varied capacities. As we brace for whatever lies beyond the horizon, one thing is certain: preparing for the ride promises to be as exciting as the journey itself.